Kilmeny Niland

A Bellbird in a Flame Tree

TAMBOURINE BOOKS
New York

Text copyright © 1989 by Angus & Robertson Publishers
Illustrations copyright © 1989 by Kilmeny Niland
First published in Australia by Angus & Robertson Publishers
a division of William Morrow & Company, Inc.,
1350 Avenue of the Americas, New York, New York 10019.
Printed in Hong Kong
First U.S. edition, 1991
10 9 8 7 6 5 4 3 2 1

Library of Congress Cataloging in Publication Data
Niland, Kilmeny.   A bellbird in a flame tree:
the Twelve days of Christmas/Kilmeny Niland.
p. cm.   Summary: On each of the twelve days of Christmas
wallabies, dingoes, lorikeets, and other animals are sent as gifts.
ISBN 0-688-10798-2 (lib.) — ISBN 0-688-10797-4 (trade)
[1. Christmas — Fiction.   2. Animals — Fiction.
3. Stories in rhyme.]   I. Twelve days of Christmas
(English folk song)   II. Title.   PZ8.3.N5668Be 1991
[E] — dc20   90-25869   CIP   AC

A Bellbird in a Flame Tree

For Leo
Hugh
Paddy
and Thomas

B+T 1-10-92 12 85

n the first day of Christmas,
my true love sent to me,

a bellbird in a flame tree.

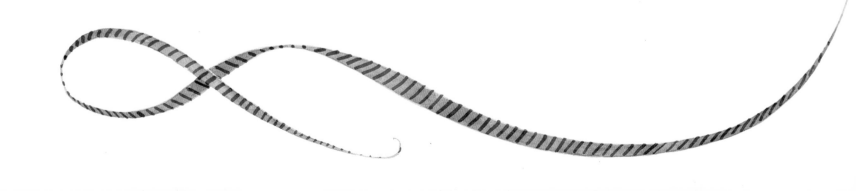

n the second day of Christmas,
my true love sent to me,

two wallabies,
and a bellbird in a flame tree.

O n the third day of Christmas,
my true love sent to me,

three lorikeets,
two wallabies,
and a bellbird in a flame tree.

n the fourth day of Christmas,
my true love sent to me,

four pelicans,
three lorikeets,
two wallabies,
and a bellbird in a flame tree.

n the fifth day of Christmas,
my true love sent to me,

five crocodiles,
four pelicans,
three lorikeets,
two wallabies,
and a bellbird in a flame tree.

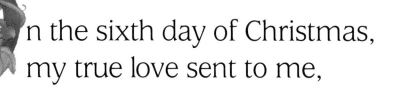

On the sixth day of Christmas,
my true love sent to me,

six penguins peeping,
five crocodiles,
four pelicans,
three lorikeets,
two wallabies,
and a bellbird in a flame tree.

On the seventh day of Christmas,
my true love sent to me,

seven mice a-marching,
six penguins peeping,
five crocodiles,
four pelicans,
three lorikeets,
two wallabies,
and a bellbird in a flame tree.

n the eighth day of Christmas,
my true love sent to me,

eight quokkas cooking,
seven mice a-marching,
six penguins peeping,
five crocodiles,
four pelicans,
three lorikeets,
two wallabies,
and a bellbird in a flame tree.

n the ninth day of Christmas,
my true love sent to me,

nine numbats knitting,
eight quokkas cooking,
seven mice a-marching,
six penguins peeping,
five crocodiles,
four pelicans,
three lorikeets,
two wallabies,
and a bellbird in a flame tree.

n the tenth day of Christmas,
my true love sent to me,

ten dingoes dancing,
nine numbats knitting,
eight quokkas cooking,
seven mice a-marching,
six penguins peeping,
five crocodiles,
four pelicans,
three lorikeets,
two wallabies,
and a bellbird in a flame tree.

n the eleventh day of Christmas,
my true love sent to me,

eleven lizards leaping,
ten dingoes dancing,
nine numbats knitting,
eight quokkas cooking,
seven mice a-marching,
six penguins peeping,
five crocodiles,
four pelicans,
three lorikeets,
two wallabies,
and a bellbird in a flame tree.

On the twelfth day of Christmas,
my true love sent to me,

twelve koalas clowning,
eleven lizards leaping,
ten dingoes dancing,
nine numbats knitting,
eight quokkas cooking,
seven mice a-marching,
six penguins peeping,
five crocodiles,
four pelicans,
three lorikeets,
two wallabies,
and a bellbird in a flame tree.